The Board of Directors

Richard A. Gilmore

I0809722

UPPER ROOM BOOKS®
NASHVILLE

THE BOARD OF DIRECTORS

Upper Room Books® website: books.upperroom.org

Cover design: GoreStudio, Inc.
Printed in the United States of America
ISBN: 978-0-8358-0883-5

Contents

What Is the Board of Directors?

Each local Emmaus community has some type of administrative structure to handle the operations. This is true of almost any organization. The size and type of an organization is important in determining its administrative structure. Within a church, there is at least one entity that serves as the policy-making body for the church. This body is generally referred to as a board of trustees or an administrative board. Some churches have more than one board, such as the board of trustees, the administrative board, the board of deacons, and so forth. The local community of the Walk to Emmaus also has a board.

Governance versus Management

Within the local Emmaus community, as within any organization, two functions are necessary for the smooth running of the organization. One is governance and the other is management. Governance is the formation of broad policy for the organization. Management is that part of the organization that sees to the day-to-day operations, being certain to function within the policies established by the governance arm.

What Is a Board?

The Emmaus board is the policy-making entity for the Emmaus organization. As such, the board is the governance arm. The governance responsibilities need to be kept separate from management duties. If the board moves into day-to-day operations, the board oversteps its responsibilities and does a disservice to the organization. The local Emmaus board members have both governance and management functions; but when meeting as a board, they need to limit their activities to governance only.

Incorporated versus Nonincorporated

The Emmaus board may be operating as a free-standing board. As such, the board needs a legal status as being incorporated. Some Emmaus boards operate under the auspices of the Conference office; some boards operate under a particular congregation. Neither of these arrangements would lead to incorporation by the Emmaus board. There are advantages and disadvantages to each type of board establishment.

501(c)3 Status

If the Emmaus board is incorporated, it should be incorporated as a 501(c)3 corporation. The 501(c)3 is a designation from the United States Internal Revenue Service (IRS) for recognition of a tax-exempt status and often is referred to as "not-for-profit." The 501(c)3 designation includes religious, educational and charitable organizations as well as a few others. Being incorporated as a 501(c)3 corporation gives the organization exemption from most federal income taxes. In addition, individuals making contributions to such a 501(c)3 corporation may count their contribution as a deduction on their individual income tax forms.

The Emmaus board may have been granted the 501(c)3 status from the Internal Revenue Service. However, if the board chooses to be incorporated, it will still need to seek incorporation through the state government. When seeking such incorporation status from the state, the application needs to include a request for tax-exempt status. The state will provide such status and will issue a tax identification number. That number will permit the Emmaus organization to purchase supplies without having to pay state sales tax.

Operating Under a Church or Congregation

For Emmaus boards that operate under the authority of a local church or larger denominational body, incorporation may not be necessary. The board needs to ascertain that the responsible agency is a 501(c)3 corporation and that the Emmaus board can exercise all the privileges of the overseeing agency such as tax deductibility for those making contributions, and a state sales tax number to exempt the Emmaus board from state sales tax on purchases.

Governing Documents

The Bylaws

Each Emmaus board has several documents that provide guidance and procedures for operating the board. *The first document is the Articles of Incorporation, sometimes referred to as the bylaws.* A copy of suggested bylaws is in *The Upper Room Handbook on Emmaus* (see pages 112–117). Attachment of a copy of the bylaws is usually required when submitting an application for incorporation to the state government.

The set of bylaws needs to contain several items. These are arranged in articles that are numbered (generally with Roman numerals), with any necessary sections under each article to further delineate the items. The sections would be numbered with Arabic numerals.

Article I would give the full name of the organization. For example: Under Article I, it would be stated that the name of this community shall be The Greater Metropolitan Area of Heaven Emmaus Community of the Universe, hereinafter referred to as the Community.

Article II would state the purpose of the organization.

Section 1 would specify that purpose.

Section 2 could be used to show that the local community is affiliated with the International Emmaus Movement, The Upper Room, Nashville, Tennessee.

Section 3 might be used to indicate the date of incorporation, which state has granted the corporation a charter, and that the corporation was granted a 501(c)3 status by the U.S. Internal Revenue Service.

Article III defines the membership of the organization.

Two sections might be helpful here. *Section 1* would include all who have completed the three-day Emmaus experience sponsored by the local community. *Section 2* would allow for people from other Emmaus events and persons who have participated in other recognized spiritual renewal three-day events to become members of the local community.

Article IV would be the board of directors.

Section 1 defines the responsibility of the board.

Section 2 defines the composition or membership of the board of directors: for example, the fifteen elected directors and the Spiritual Director of the community. Generally, it is specified that each of these persons has one vote on the board. If there are other persons that are board members, that is specified in this section. It is possible that other persons may have a seat on the board by virtue of their position. An example of this might be a community that holds all of their Emmaus functions at a local church and the community allows the church to have a pastor from the church staff to serve on the board. These persons serve *ex officio*, that is, by virtue of the office. These persons are not elected; they serve because they hold the position in the church.

Many people associate *ex officio* and non-voting as being the same. According to the dictionary and to *Robert's Rules of Order*, the two are not associated. All directors on the board (elected as well as *ex officio*) are full voting members unless the bylaws explicitly limit the voting privileges. Persons should not be disenfranchised because of the mechanism of being seated on the board.

Section 3 defines the term of office for the directors and how they are elected. If there are fifteen elected board members that serve three-year staggered terms, this must be specified in this section. It could be stated that the directors are elected for three-year terms in three classes, each having five members. This section needs to address the issue of succession of board members. If they cannot succeed themselves, how many years must they wait to be eligible for reelection, if reelection is allowed? If reelection is allowed, a waiting period of at least two years is helpful. This assures opportunities for others to serve the Emmaus community in this leadership capacity.

This section also needs to specify when the term of office begins and when it ends; for example, the term begins October 15 and ends October 14. It is advisable to avoid the end of February as a starting or ending date because of February's added day every four years (Leap Year). If there are any exceptions to the ending date because of some later article and section of the bylaws, it is well to state that at this point.

Section 4 should fully describe the process for election of board members. This includes the mechanism of balloting (by mail, certified mail, details of how to submit the ballot, etc.). The number of nominees for the ballot is to be specified as well as how many are to be elected. The ballot may require seven names in order to elect five directors. The location and date of availability of the ballot are to be specified.

For example, the ballot may be provided in the October issue of the community newsletter. The section must specify a date by when ballots are to be received for them to be included in the counting. The last part of this section specifies how to determine which five are elected. The simplest approach is to elect the five receiving the highest number of votes.

Section 5 deals with board meetings. State here the frequency of board meetings, such as monthly or quarterly. Make provision for calling special meetings. This could appear as a separate section or as part of this section.

There should be two mechanisms for calling special meetings of the Emmaus board. The chair of the board has the right to call special meetings. A defined number of directors (frequently two-thirds of the total number) can call for a special meeting. It is helpful if this number is the same as the quorum, thus assuring there is a quorum for the called meeting. Outline provisions for proper notification for special meetings in this section. Three calendar days' notice is customary. Special meetings are limited to discussion of only the item(s) contained in the request for the meeting.

Section 6 presents the quorum. Stating a specific number of voting members for a quorum is better than a percentage. The percentage may result in a fraction of a member and then it must be resolved how to handle the fraction. The quorum is the minimum number of qualified persons present in order for the board to conduct business. If your quorum is 10 and 10 qualified persons are present, business can be conducted. If one of these persons leaves, the meeting is ended at that point for lack of a quorum.

Section 7 is a good place to present information about the past chair serving an additional year on the board, if the community decides that is valuable. This is a recommended procedure because it assists the new board chair in the transition to this area of responsibility. Additionally, the past board chair is a good source of information about past board actions so that the new chair is not inadvertently trying to do something the board had previously accomplished.

Section 8 presents the procedures to be followed to fill a vacancy on the board that occurs between elections. It is common practice to have the chair nominate a person for the vacant position and have the board vote on the nomination. This section should indicate that a person elected by the board to fill an unexpired term is eligible for election to a full term when that seat is up for reelection.

Section 9 contains information about standing committees. This could be set as a separate article. The committees must be named, information given as to how the chairs are determined (they should be board members), and either what the responsibilities are or where the responsibilities can be found. A list of committees is provided in Table 1 of this book on page 28.

Section 10 delineates the nominating committee and its responsibilities if it is not a standing committee. This information is to include the number of people on the committee, how many can be board members, and how many must be non-board members. How the committee is appointed is to be specified as well as when it is to be formed. There should be a date by when the committee's report is to be submitted to the board.

Section 11 should state that the chair of the board is an *ex officio* member of each committee of the board.

Article V deals with the officers of the board.

Section 1 states the officers by position—chair, secretary, treasurer, etc. This section defines the line of responsibility for chairing the board meeting in the event the chair is not present.

Section 2 provides information that determines when the officers are elected and who elects them. The board members elect their own officers. The date of assuming the responsibilities of the office are to be specified. The transition is easily handled if the transfer of the responsibilities is effective with the close of the meeting where the officers are elected.

This section is also the place to define succession of officers. If the board officers are to be selected only from those directors elected by the community, specify that in this section.

Section 3 is the place to provide information about directors who are elected by the board. Most Emmaus communities elect the community Spiritual Director on an annual basis, and the board elects this individual.

Article VI presents information about the three-day Walk to Emmaus event.

Section 1 states that the community will conduct the three day (72-hour) experience according to the model as defined by the International Director of the Walk to Emmaus and as presented in The Upper Room Handbook on Emmaus.

Section 2 delineates the board's oversight of the local community.

Section 3 specifies the selection of the Spiritual Director for each three-day Walk to Emmaus.

Section 4 describes the selection of the Lay Director for each Walk to Emmaus.

Section 5 has information about the team selection committee. Specified in this section are the composition of the committee, the appointment of the committee members, and the responsibilities of the committee.

Section 6 deals with the clergy nominees for each Emmaus weekend.

Section 7 specifies board approval of the proposed team members and alternates, both lay and clergy.

Article VII deals with amendments to the bylaws and should include voting on amendments by the community.

Section 1 describes how proposed amendments are to be presented, to whom, and when. There should be a delay of at least one meeting between receipt of the proposed amendment and the board voting on that proposal. This time line is to be detailed in this section. The standard procedure is to have the amendment presented (read) at one meeting, but with no discussion or action taken until the next meeting.

Section 2 describes the approval process. Since the board must approve the amendment, it is best to state that the amendment must receive an affirmative vote of three-fourths of the voting members present at a duly constituted meeting. The next step in the process is to have the community vote on the proposed amendment. This should be accomplished by a mail ballot. The community can approve the amendment by a simple majority affirmative vote of those casting a ballot. A deadline for receipt of ballots from the community must be specified.

At the first meeting of the board following the deadline for receipt of the community ballots, the board certifies the results of the community vote. The results of the voting must be reported to the community. This is best accomplished by a notice in the community newsletter.

Section 3 presents information about the effective date of any amendment. This could be a statement that an amendment becomes effective with the board's certification. Some amendments, however, may include an effective date as a part of the amendment.

Additional articles and sections may be included in the bylaws to assist the Emmaus board and the local Emmaus community in their operation. Consider the needs for communities that cover a large geographic area. There may be one board, but individual towns within the area may have local gatherings and promotion of reunion groups. Local groups may present the three-day Walk to Emmaus event. They may have a local steering committees operating under the jurisdiction of the one board.

If this is the case, it may be helpful to have the chair of the local group serve as a member of the board. In such situations, detail the mechanism for this in the bylaws.

The 501(c)3 Application

A second governing document is the 501(c)3 application and the IRS regulatory statutes. These statutes must be followed rigorously. Failure to do so could result in the loss of the 501(c)3 status. The primary issues in these statutes are the annual report to the IRS, the annual financial report, and the disposition of funds. Each 501(c)3 corporation is required to prepare an annual financial report and to provide copies of that report to anyone who requests it. The disposition of funds has two aspects: (1) that a 501(c)3 corporation can make contributions only to other 501(c)3 corporations, and (2) that if the corporation decides to cease operations, all assets are to be delivered to another 501(c)3 corporation.

State Statutes of Incorporation

The third governing document is the rules or statutes of the state where the board is incorporated. Generally, states require such corporations to file an annual report and to name a registered agent. The registered agent is the contact person for all governmental purposes.

Rules of Operation

The fourth governing document is the rules of operation. This is not required, but certainly is very helpful to the Emmaus board in carrying out its functions. The rules of operation are defined by the board for the operation of the board. These rules of operation do not need approval by anyone except the board. These rules should be relatively simple to change. The change could be approved by a simple majority of those eligible to vote when the voting is conducted at a duly called meeting with a quorum present.

The Covenant Letter

The fifth governing document for the Emmaus board is the Covenant Letter. The International Director of the Walk to Emmaus provides this document and authorizes the local Emmaus community to offer the Walk to Emmaus. A detailed discussion about the Covenant Letter is found on pages 31–33.

Members of the Board of Directors

The members of the board are commonly referred to as directors. Other terms that may be used are *trustees, regents,* or *solicitors.* The term *directors* is best for Emmaus boards, since this term is readily recognized and rarely needs definition when used.

All directors are elected from the membership at large. The eligibility requirements and the election process are defined in the bylaws. The number of directors will be specified in the bylaws. Each director serves a specified term as directed in the bylaws. Allowing a board member to be reelected to a second consecutive term is delineated in the bylaws. If it is allowed, the bylaws should specify the number of terms for succession.

Most Emmaus communities do not allow succession of board directors. This assists in providing opportunities for broad representation of the community on the board. Many Emmaus communities have a board of directors with fifteen members elected at large plus one to three members that are elected by the board or serve as defined in the bylaws.

The fifteen members elected at large generally are elected five per year, each serving a three-year term. This provides the opportunity to maintain continuity for the board, yet allows new members to be added each year. Such a procedure sustains the viability of the board and simultaneously maintains the vitality of the board.

One of the remaining directors is the community Spiritual Director, who is elected annually by the board. The procedure for this is defined in the bylaws and should include information about allowance for succession.

When the Emmaus board elects new officers (see page 18), it is common to have the outgoing chair serve an additional year on the board. This needs to be delineated in the bylaws. Thus, an outgoing chair who simultaneously completes the three-year term of at-large election would serve a fourth year on the board, assuming the bylaws so prescribe. Thus, this person serves one year on the board, not as an elected member but as a bylaw-defined member.

Some Emmaus communities have a third director who is not elected at large. These communities separate the functions of the Chair of the Board and the Community Lay Director. For these communities, the Community Lay Director is elected annually by the board, much as the Community Spiritual Director is elected annually by the board. In these instances, the Community Lay Director is not the board chair and is not eligible to be elected as board chair. The specifics for this position are specified in the bylaws.

Accountability of the Directors

The directors serving on the Emmaus board have several avenues of accountability. *The first avenue of accountability is to those who elected the directors. Thus, the directors are accountable to the Emmaus community at large.* As such, the board members need to be responsive to the community members and any comments brought by them. This is an excellent example of leaders leading through serving those they are trying to lead. This is the method of leadership taught by Jesus Christ as evidenced in Matthew 20:25-28.

The next avenue of accountability for the directors is the official in the state government who granted the corporation its status. Most states require the submission of an annual report that specifies who is the registered agent for the corporation and the address for contacting this individual. The registered agent is the person who serves as custodian of the official seal of the corporation (if there is one), and also serves as the person to receive official documents from various government agencies.

An additional avenue of accountability for the directors of the Emmaus board is the IRS (Internal Revenue Service). The board is required to meet the IRS statutes for 501(c)3 corporations. In general, the minimum is to file the annual IRS report. If the board has any paid employees, the reporting requirements become more complex. For those Emmaus boards that are 501(c)3 corporations and that do have one or more paid employees, the board should seek advice and direction from a local tax accountant or tax attorney.

In some instances the board of directors may he accountable to those persons who make donations to the Emmaus board. The directors should be very cautious about placing themselves in such a situation. If a person offers to make a contribution to the Emmaus board and specifies what is to be done with the funds, the board has two options: to accept the funds or not. If the board does accept the funds, then the board is obligated to use the funds as specified by the donor. This makes the board of directors accountable to the donor.

Failure to maintain this type of accountability presents several problematic situations. The donor may request to have the money returned, with interest, and the donor would have the legal system on his side in support of such a request. Should the board deny the request, litigation would probably ensue, which would be costly for the board. Such litigation, if the board were to lose the case, could result in the loss of the board's 501(c)3 status.

The final avenue of accountability for the directors of the Emmaus board is to the International Director of the Walk to Emmaus. The board annually completes a *Covenant Letter* (details are found on page 31) with the International Director, and this obligates the board of directors to function in accordance with that agreement.

Officers of the Board

The bylaws of the Emmaus board specify the officers that are to serve. The bylaws will indicate each office and provide brief descriptions of the responsibilities of each office. In addition, the bylaws will designate the line of responsibility in chairing board meetings in the absence of the elected chair.

Election of Officers

Officers of the board are elected from the seated board members, and they are elected by the board of directors. Some Emmaus communities have a provision in their bylaws that only the board members who were elected by the community can serve as officers of the board. The bylaws will specify when the election of officers is to be held, and this usually is an annual process. The nomination procedures should be specified in the bylaws. The rules of operation should not address these issues since the rules of operation are easily changed by the board, whereas the bylaws are not easily changed.

The minimum list of officers should include the chair, a secretary, and a treasurer. Some Emmaus communities have a vice-chair position. Additional officers may be included based on the particular needs of a community.

Terms of Office

In general, the term of office for each board member is one year. The advantages of one-year terms for the officers far outweigh the disadvantages. The main disadvantage is the need to have the election each year. While the procedure may be simple, the process can become protracted.

One advantage of annual terms for the officers is that we are a very mobile society, and businesses do make large changes in numbers of personnel. The one-year term of office is very amenable to such fluctuations. Another advantage of one-year terms is the development of leaders for the Emmaus community. Leadership development is part of the intent of the Walk to Emmaus, and the local board of directors should be intentional about this. The officers of the board should spend time during their term of office in training and developing people to take their place.

Succession of Officers

Can Emmaus board officers succeed themselves? The answer is yes. The better question is, *should* they succeed themselves? Effective arguments can be made for both sides of this issue. Many Emmaus communities will allow the chair to serve no more than two consecutive terms. One reason for this is the desire to retain an especially effective leader. Limiting the incumbent to one additional term does promote the aspect of offering leadership opportunities to others. Mandating two years would be a disservice to the Emmaus board and the Emmaus community in the event of unforeseen circumstances.

The other board officers could serve successive terms for the length of tenure on the board without any negative ramification for the board. If this is to be the case, it must be specified in the bylaws.

Duties of Board Members

The Emmaus board members are expected to conduct their duties faithfully, sincerely, and in a cooperative manner. The members of the Emmaus community who elected the board members have the right to expect that the board members will act responsibly.

The first duty of the Emmaus board member is to attend the board meetings. Prior to being elected, the potential board member knows when the board meets and should consider that time commitment before allowing his or her name to be listed on the ballot. This is part of the responsibility which Jesus mentioned in Luke 14:28-30 when he talks about counting the cost before you embark on something. Each board member is relying on the other board members to be present at meetings so the quorum can be met. Without a quorum, the board cannot conduct business. Another reason to attend board meetings is that each board member is held accountable for the board decisions, whether or not the member was present at the meeting when the decision was made.

It is a duty of board members to be informed of what is happening at the board meetings as well as what is happening in the local community. In addition, the board member needs to be informed of what is occurring in Emmaus at the International headquarters as well as the international scene. Board members are to be sufficiently informed so they can direct questions to the proper persons for response or make the appropriate contacts to get answers to the questions.

Board members have the duty to participate in discussions. The people who elected the board member expect that participation on the part of the board member will occur. Participation occurs on three levels. The first level is in discussion of the issue. The second is in casting a vote (as opposed to abstaining) on the motion. The third level is implementation and supporting the decision of the board on the issue. This has nothing to do with how the board member voted on the issue. *Once the decision is made by the board, each board member has the duty to support that decision fully.*

Another duty of board members is to exercise independent judgment. The Emmaus community elects board members who will carefully, and prayerfully, think for themselves as individuals. While this is very important, it comes with some stringent requirements. As board members exercise independent judgment, the judgment has to be based on what is best for the organization. Thus, board members, at all times, must act for the sole benefit and interest of the corporation. This is commonly referred to as the fiduciary relation or the fiduciary responsibility.

One board duty is delegation. As was discussed in the early pages of this book, the board operates at the level of governance. The board delegates the day-to-day business to others, and hence the management aspect is conducted by others outside of board meetings. This becomes a very fine line to walk for Emmaus board members because they serve on both sides of the line. The board meetings are to be preserved for governance functions and the management functions are to be left for other times. Information about the management functions is presented later in this book.

Board members have the duty to be loyal. This loyalty is to the board, the community, the various governance documents, and to the principles, goals, and interests of the corporation. If one comes to the board meetings with her or his own agenda or makes a determined effort to "do it my way," he is not being loyal to the duty of a board member. This loyalty to set aside personal desire for the sake of the corporation is part of the fiduciary responsibility mentioned above.

A significant duty of a board member is confidentiality. There are two areas where confidentiality plays a role. The first area involves persons. If a problem occurs in the Emmaus community or at an Emmaus function and it is brought to the board, that problem and the names of all persons involved is confidential to the board—and to the board only. Board members are to refrain from any indications about the issue outside of board meetings.

The second area of confidentiality involves notification. If board members agree at a board meeting that member A will make an announcement about an issue, then all other board members are to respect that confidentiality and let member A make the announcement. If member B decides to share the information with someone before A announces it, then B has violated the confidentiality.

Committees of the Board

The Emmaus board has the right to establish committees to assist the board with its functions. There are three types of committees. These are special (or *ad hoc*), standing (or permanent), and executive committees. Each type of committee can provide a valuable service to the board, but having each type of committee may not be necessary. In some circumstances a committee could prove not to be beneficial.

Special Committees (ad hoc)

Special committees are established for a specific task. The committee is given a written charge of what it is to do, and a time limit is specified. When the committee work is finished, or when the time limit has passed, the committee ceases to function. Time limit extensions can be given by the board; but if they are given, they need to be specified in writing so current and future board members will have a record of the change in the time limit.

An example of a special committee could be a celebration committee. The board decides to celebrate the tenth anniversary of the local Emmaus community. The board establishes a special committee for the celebration. The charge to the committee includes the date of the celebration and the committee is to make recommendations about a site for the event and all the details of the event, including projected costs. The committee is given six months to complete its task.

When the committee completes its efforts, it submits a written report to the board. The board may accept the report, modify the report, or disregard the report and start over. The board could accept the report and give the same committee a new charge to implement the report and prepare the celebration.

Standing Committees (permanent)

Committees of this type have recurring functions and are defined in the bylaws. Some of the details of the way the committee operates may be in the standing rules.

An example of a standing committee may be the nominating committee. This committee is to prepare a slate of candidates that will be presented to the Emmaus community to elect new members of the board. In general, this committee would conduct its activities once per year. The committee meets to recommend persons for consideration. The persons the committee approves are personally contacted by one or more members of the committee to determine that individual's interest, willingness, and availability.

In general, if five persons are to be elected, at least seven names should appear on the ballot. The voting procedures are defined in the bylaws. If you are electing five members and only have five names on the ballot, the voting process must be carried out as specified in the bylaws. While this may seem to be an extravagant expense of money and time, it is required to be done, and the government agencies overseeing the operations of such corporations may conduct audits of compliance with your bylaws.

Executive Committee

The executive committee, if there is one, must be specified in the bylaws. The executive committee functions in two areas.

The first area is to deal with issues presented to the board to determine how they should be handled. It could be determined that it is a board function, and that item would be placed on the agenda for the next board meeting. The executive committee could determine that the issue would best be handled by a standing committee, and that item is referred out to committee.

The second area for the executive committee is to function as the board between board meetings. When this does occur, the executive committee exercises the full power and authority of the whole board. For Emmaus communities, the board generally meets monthly; thus there would not be a need for an executive committee.

Composition of Committees

Special committees and standing committees should each have at least one board member (preferably only one board member), and the remaining members should be from the Emmaus community at large. For special committees, the board chair may name all the committee members or may name only the board member to be on the committee. In the latter situation, the board member then selects the remaining committee members.

Standing committees should have a board member as chair and the remaining members selected by the committee chair. The executive committee, if one is used, is composed exclusively of board members. Emmaus community members at large are not to be named to the executive committee.

Committee Size

The optimal size of a committee is three to seven members. If the task of the committee is extensive, subcommittees can be established. For a subcommittee, a member of the parent committee serves as chair. This provides representation for each subcommittee at the parent committee meeting.

Records

Special committees prepare a written report and submit that report to the board. The report should be dated and should have the signature and typed (printed) name of the chair of the committee.

Standing committees and executive committees are to submit detailed minutes to the board. These minutes are to be dated and should carry the signature and typed name of the secretary of the committee or the chair of the committee.

Why Have Committees?

The purpose of the Walk to Emmaus is to develop leaders for the church. In the Emmaus community, committees are the only place where leadership development is actually put into practice. Committees are small groups of people working together for a common goal. A good example of this is the fact that Jesus Christ used a small group of twelve as the primary training group.

Committees provide the opportunity for people to get involved in what is going on rather than just attending events. Without this involvement, the members of the Emmaus community will gradually fade away. Having people involved in committees gives the people a sense of belonging. It also provides the members of the Emmaus community a broader exposure to all that needs to be done to maintain the community as a dynamic, supportive group.

Committees handle the day-to-day operations of the organization. As such, committees are the management arm of the organization. Having committees completes the organizational structure of the Emmaus community. The board serves as the governance arm, and the committees serve as the management arm.

Committees provide the opportunity to spread the work among more people. This reduces the workload for any one person and helps many people learn about the various facets of the Walk to Emmaus. Committees also provide a unique opportunity for a variety of people to share supportively with each other the enhancing of the Christian walk, both for the Emmaus pilgrims and for the individual committee members.

How Do Committees Operate?

Each member of the board of directors is chair of a committee. One exception to this is the board chair. The board chair is an *ex officio* member of all committees. *Ex officio* means by virtue of the office. Thus the person holding the office of chair of the board is a member of every committee of the board. *Ex officio* members are full voting members of the committee unless the bylaws specify some other role for *ex officio* members.

Some board committee responsibilities are very extensive. As such, several subcommittees are very helpful and the chair of the committee is highly encouraged to establish subcommittees. This provides the opportunity to have more people involved.

Committee Assignments

If one considers all the functions of the local Emmaus community, that will provide a solid list of needed committees. Two examples of committee assignments for board members are presented in Table 1 (see page 28). Each of the examples in Table 1 is used by different Emmaus communities. Some communities have added a community training or education committee.

Each board member chairs a committee. The assignments are made by the board chair. The board member selects the remaining committee members from the community at large. These committees carry out the functions assigned, which allows the board to concentrate the efforts on governing the local community and overseeing the quality of the program.

Possible Committee Assignments

Table 1

Example A	*Example B*
Registration	Registration
Transportation	Transportation/Housing
Facility/Set up	Facility Set up
Agape	Agape
Kitchen	Kitchen
Literature	Literature
Music	Music/Entertainment
Entertainment	
Candlelight/Sponsor's Hour	Candlelight/Sponsor's Hour
Group Reunions	Group Reunions
Gatherings	Gatherings
Newsletter	Newsletter
Prison Ministries	Emerging Ministries
Team Selection	Team Selection
Prayer	Fourth Day

One Committee: An Example

The monthly gatherings of the local Emmaus community have several functions that need attention. There is one board member who is responsible for the committee in charge of gatherings. The various details that the committee has to deal with are: location, fourth day speaker, clergy person, music, Communion (elements/utensils/servers), offering (collection, counting, submission to treasurer), to treasurer, moderator (or master of ceremonies), prayer, scripture reading, child care.

While the one board person could handle all ten of these functions, it is much easier to have the committee provide the service to accomplish everything. The board person could have a committee of ten persons to assist. The ten persons on the committee could each chair a subcommittee that is responsible for one of the functions. Since the gatherings are held monthly, one subcommittee is arranging for the clergy for each month. Similarly, each subcommittee is making arrangements for their area of responsibility for the year.

This arrangement allows the board person responsible for gatherings to oversee what is going on and having others do the work. As the subcommittees and the parent committee conduct their activities, the board person can determine who is taking a leadership role and who is just along for the ride.

If each subcommittee has three members to assist the subcommittee chair, then there would be forty people involved in making arrangements for the gatherings, and that does not include the board person who chairs the parent committee. It is imperative to remember that these forty people are responsible to get others to do the function at the gatherings.

When the board meets, the board members report the activities of their committees and subcommittees. The board person responsible for gatherings would provide a report of when and where each gathering would be held. It would not be necessary to take the time of the board meeting to delineate all the details of each gathering.

Covenant Letter

Each local Emmaus community is asked to complete a *Covenant Letter* each year. The *Covenant Letter* is provided from the office of the International Director of the Walk to Emmaus. The Covenant Letter is a covenant between the board of the local Emmaus community and The Upper Room. This covenant provides several things that the board agrees to do and several things The Upper Room agrees to do.

The local Emmaus community commitments include having a governing board that is elected by the members of the community. This local governing body will operate in accordance with The Upper Room Walk to Emmaus guidelines and will maintain effective communication with the office of the International Director of the Walk to Emmaus.

The local governing body agrees to conduct the three-phase method of the Walk to Emmaus according to The Upper Room Walk to Emmaus model as presented in *The Upper Room Handbook on Emmaus* and as interpreted by The Upper Room manuals. The three phases of the Walk to Emmaus are pre-event, event, and post-event.

The pre-event phase includes an effective recruitment process with proper interpretation. In addition, there is to be proper and effective preparation for all participants and the team members for their involvement in the three-day Walk to Emmaus experience.

The event phase is to be provided as separate three-day events for men and for women. These events are to be conducted in accordance with the manuals and talk outlines that are available from The Upper Room.

The post-event phase is a four-pronged effort that includes the local community providing encouragement for and assistance in getting Emmaus participants involved in their local church. The community will actively promote, support, and encourage group reunions and monthly gatherings. The last part of this four-pronged effort is to present leadership training for all Emmaus participants as a means of providing spiritual renewal for the church.

The local governing body and its community are to intentionally foster interdenominational and interracial participation. In this process, the local community is to foster a spirit of Christian tolerance and unity. The local community also is to foster an openness to diversity and mainstream theological balance.

The local governing body is to maintain regular communication with denominational leaders and other church officials about the activities and results of the local Emmaus undertakings. The local governing body is to strive to work with denominational structures and to be an effective servant of the church.

The local governing body is to authorize and to have conducted a yearly review of the finances of the local group. This review must be performed by someone other than the treasurer of the local community. Copies of this annual review are to be made available to persons who request such information.

The local governing body, in keeping with the Emmaus focus, will develop sponsorship in the local community so that pilgrims who are actively involved in a local church are the ones invited to participate in the Walk to Emmaus. The local governing body will support the equal commitment rule (explained in the next section of this book) and foster the use of this rule within the local Emmaus community.

The local governing body will keep the local Emmaus community informed about and support the Emmaus Funding Plan.

This plan requests each local Emmaus community to contribute five dollars for each new participant following each Walk to Emmaus weekend event. These funds are to be submitted to the Office of the International Director of the Walk to Emmaus to be used exclusively for The Upper Room's efforts in support of the Walk to Emmaus.

As part of the covenant of the *Covenant Letter,* The Upper Room grants to the local governing body the right to use the term *Walk to Emmaus.* The Walk to Emmaus is a program that is copyrighted, and The Upper Room owns the copyright. The *Covenant Letter* is the written permission for the local Emmaus board to use the copyrighted material, but it does not provide permission to copy any of the material.

The Office of the International Director of the Walk to Emmaus will provide support to the local Emmaus community. This support will include guidance and consultation, interpretive materials on Emmaus, and direction and leadership for starting an Emmaus community. In addition, printed materials for use in leading all aspects of the various phases of the Walk to Emmaus can be purchased through this office. Also, the office of the International Director will serve as the contact for providing resource persons for leadership training for the local Emmaus community. This office will additionally serve as the coordinating point for networking with the Emmaus movement as it expands throughout the world.

The Upper Room will offer support to Emmaus participants for their Fourth Day activities. The Upper Room produces print, video, and experiential resources that can be used to strengthen the spiritual life. Upon request, information about these resources will be provided.

The Upper Room will provide local Emmaus communities a discount on books purchased from The Upper Room that are used for book tables at Emmaus events. The Upper Room International Emmaus office will strive to maintain regular communication with each local Emmaus community.

Equal Commitment Rule

The *Covenant Letter* contains the following statement regarding married couples and their participation as pilgrims on the Walk to Emmaus weekend event: "Married couples are encouraged to make an equal commitment to participate in the Walk to Emmaus." This does not mean that Emmaus is only for married couples. Emmaus embraces persons regardless of their marital status. The rule reflects the concern for and the desire about the effect of Emmaus participation on marriage and the family.

Emmaus does not want to become a wedge in any marriage. The equal commitment rule helps to guard against this. The Walk to Emmaus can be a launching pad for new commitments and directions in a marriage. These potentials may not be realized by the couple at the time of presentation of information about the Walk. The equal involvement of both members or parties of the couple is necessary for the marriage to derive this potential. Thus the rule is provided to assist Emmaus in strengthening the marriage and the family bonds and to avoid those practices that are known to potentially adversely affect a marriage.

Emmaus can be a vital agent in strengthening the spiritual bond in a marriage. Both members of the couple should be approached at the same time when the Walk to Emmaus is being presented and applications are being offered. At this point in the conversation, there should be strong encouragement for the couple to make an equal commitment to participate. The equal involvement of couples will strengthen the Emmaus movement and will help strengthen the local church.

Experience has shown that the application of the equal commitment rule has resulted in the active participation in Emmaus and the local church of both husbands and wives who probably would not have attended the Walk to Emmaus event otherwise. These persons made the commitment to attend because their spouse wanted to attend. While the initial motive may have been to help the spouse, they have found that the Emmaus experience has been a vital ingredient in their Christian growth. The weekend experience became a very personal event in their lives.

The equal commitment rule is not intended to be a barrier to prevent a person from attending the Walk to Emmaus if his or her spouse will not attend. Individual circumstances may prevent a husband or a wife from attending the same set of walks. This should not be used as a reason to speak to them individually. The presentation of the Walk to Emmaus still should be made simultaneously to both parties of the couple. This allows the couple to discuss their involvement and to examine their schedules before making the commitment to attend. There is nothing wrong with the couple delaying to a later date so they can take advantage of the same set of walks. Let the couple make that decision.

> It is important that the wisdom of the rule be honored in Emmaus communities. The equal commitment rule represents a practical ideal to which Emmaus Communities should be committed and toward which sponsors should work in all cases. It is important to remember, however, that the equal commitment rule represents wisdom, not law. There is a place for reasonable exceptions. Exceptions can be made by Boards of Directors when there is no possibility of the participation of both spouses and there

is reason for assurance that the marriage will not be adversely affected by the participation of only one spouse.
(from *The Upper Room Handbook on Emmaus,* p. 27)

There may be instances in which a couple has never shared in religious participation during their marriage. The two have agreed that the one spouse could be as active as he or she wants and the other spouse accepts this without any conflict. This is a part of the reality of their marriage and they have been able to cope with it.

How are these situations handled? The equal commitment rule is to be applied with grace. The local Emmaus board must prayerfully establish the guidelines for implementation of this rule and any exceptions. The registrar most likely will be the person having to implement the board decision on this, but the board needs to establish the ways and means of implementation so the registrar is protected.

Other Concerns

A new community will generally conduct four to six walks (two to three men's walks and two to three women's walks) before they make the transition to having a board of directors. The International Director will work with each new community to assist in this transition. The Director will generally arrange for a community training event prior to the new community becoming a board.

From Steering Committee to Board

How to make the transition is more involved. A set of bylaws must be developed. This first set of bylaws needs to include the initial election process for all fifteen board members and must provide for staggered terms. This will entail having one group of five board members elected for one year, a second group of five elected for two years, and the third group of five elected for three years. Subsequent elections would each be for three-year terms. It may be helpful to allow those elected to a one-year term to be reelected to a full three-year term. If such a provision is to be allowed, it must be included in the bylaws and clearly defined as being only for those initially elected to a one-year term at the origin of the board.

How do you decide who will be on the ballot for a one-year, two-year, or three-year term? The individuals should be asked to serve in the specific capacity. If the issue cannot be resolved by this method, then the next best thing is to elect the fifteen directors and then randomly assign them to the one-, two-, or three-year term. Procedures are available to use a statistically random process in conjunction with a table of random numbers.

Another possibility is to have the terms be part of the balloting process. The ballot would list the names alphabetically and the five candidates receiving the highest number of votes would serve three years. The second group of five candidates with the next highest vote totals would serve two years, and the third group of five candidates with the next highest vote totals would serve one year.

It is advantageous if the first board chair is a person serving a two- or three-year term on the board. The first board chair is going to be quite busy in the transition and development of the board. It will take the board more than a year to settle in. This is not meant to have the first board chair elected for a two-year term, but it does allow the board the opportunity to reelect the first board chair to a second term.

The first responsibility of the new board is to meet and elect officers. The first board meeting is convened by the head of the steering committee unless that person was elected to the board. In that event, a person serving on the steering committee who was not elected to the board should then convene the first meeting of the board. In the case where all steering committee members are elected to the board, the chair of the steering committee serves as the convener and guides the board through the election of the chair. Once the board has elected the first chair, the board chair immediately assumes responsibility for the remainder of the meeting.

The next order of business is to elect the remaining board officers from the seated board members. Following this, the board needs to elect the community Spiritual Director. If the board has not been divided into classes for the staggered terms, that action becomes the next order of business.

The board's next agenda item is to assign the board members as chairs of the standing committees. This appointment of committee chairs is made by the board chair. The next agenda item is to set regular board meeting dates and times. The meetings may be specified in the bylaws; but if the bylaws only state the board meets monthly, the date must be determined by the board. It is most helpful to have a regular meeting date for the board; for example, the second Friday of each month. This makes it easier for board members to plan their time, and it is a great help to board members in trying to remember when the meetings are held.

Each board member should be provided The Upper Room Handbook on Emmaus. The board members need to read this document and understand it. It is an excellent source of information about the responsibilities of each standing committee that the board member chairs.

The new board needs to establish a date for a community training day. This event is to help educate everyone in the community about the events of the Walk to Emmaus and the reasons why things are done the way they are. This will be an opportunity for the new Emmaus community to gain an understanding of the model of the Walk to Emmaus. The new community should contact the office of the International Director of the Walk to Emmaus to arrange for a person to present this community training.

Family Members Serving Together

Each board needs to carefully consider the question of family members serving together on the board. Each board member must act independently. Having two members from the same family serving simultaneously may not be a problem for the two members, but it may provide the appearance of a problem for the community members. The board may decide that family members are not to serve simultaneously on the board so that there is a broader community involvement on the board. The bylaws need to be specific on this issue if the board limits one family member serving at a time.

Insurance Considerations

The board needs to carefully consider the issue of liability insurance. The facility where the three-day event is held may have liability insurance as part of the fee that is paid for using the facility. The board needs to clarify the extent of coverage that is provided and who is covered under this arrangement. Where walks are held in local churches, that local church's liability policy may provide the coverage needed.

Even though the host facility has liability coverage, the members of the board may be subjected to litigation. The board needs to review their local situation carefully and be certain that adequate liability protection is available.

For boards that are incorporated, there should be serious consideration given to having directors and officers (D & 0) insurance. This provides an extra measure of protection for individual board members.

Richard A. Gilmore, a professional educator, is a member of the Northern Illinois Emmaus Board and the International Emmaus Steering Committee.